Restrictions on Business Mobility

Restrictions on Business Mobility

A Study in Political Rhetoric and Economic Reality

Richard B. McKenzie

American Enterprise Institute for Public Policy Research
Washington, D.C.

Richard B. McKenzie is professor of economics at Clemson University.

$\mathcal{1}$

HC 110
D5
M23

In developing this monograph, I am indebted to Yale Brozen, Thomas Schaap, and Clinton Whitehurst for valuable research suggestions and comments on arguments presented. I am also indebted to Mary Ann McKenzie for editorial assistance, to Imre Karafaith and Gene Wilson for research assistance, and Dinah Lanning for typing the manuscript. Finally, the previous research of C. L. Jusenius and L. C. Ledebur, cited in the text, was especially valuable in organizing the empirical examination of restrictions on business mobility.

Richard B. McKenzie

Library of Congress Catalog Card No. 79–12342

ISBN 0–8447–3338–5

AEI Studies 235

Printed in the United States of America

CONTENTS

AUG 5 1986

LIST OF FIGURES

1
Introduction

Business movements from old to new locations—from one part of the country to another part—are adjustments to economic forces and are to be expected in any large and dynamic economy. Nonetheless, such relocations can spawn political protests by workers and communities who are left behind, who believe they have been "wronged," and who, consequently, believe business movements should be restricted.

In recent years, bills have been introduced in state legislatures and in the U.S. Congress that would impose serious restrictions on business movements. Such proposals, if implemented, would bring about a dramatic and far-reaching shift in domestic economic policy and would substantially increase state and federal government supervision of business decisions. This study evaluates the case for and consequences of business mobility.

Description of Proposed Restrictions

The general purpose of the legislation that has already been passed in Maine and of proposals submitted in the Ohio and New Jersey general assemblies and in Congress in prior years is to remedy what has been called the "runaway plant phenomenon."[1] Proposals to restrict business mobility tend to have several important features. First, a government agency would be established to investigate business movements and rule on the appropriateness of business reloca-

---

[1] State of Maine, *Severance Pay Law*, Title 26 Section 625-A, pp. 83–85; State of Ohio, General Assembly, S. B. no. 337, Regular Session, 1977–1978; State of New Jersey, Assembly, *Employment Relocation Assistance Act*, no. 61, 1978 Session; and U.S. Congress, *National Employment Priorities Act of 1977*, p. 6.

1

tion. For example, the National Employment Priorities Act of 1977, introduced in the last Congress, would have established within the Department of Labor a National Employment Relocation Administration to conduct "investigations and issue reports on any proposed closing or transfer of operations of . . . a business with 50 or more employees" and "to determine the extent of the employment loss of the individuals and communities involved [and] whether such closing or transfer is without adequate justification."[2] In the Employment Relocation Assistance Act, pending before the New Jersey Assembly in 1978, the supervising state agency would be known as the Division of Business Relocation and have responsibilities similar to those of the proposed federal agency.[3]

Second, proposals to restrict business movements would impose penalties on firms whose moves are deemed "without adequate justification." The Ohio proposal, for instance, would have required a business that relocates to pay the employees left behind severance pay equal to one week's pay for each year of service and to pay the community it leaves an amount equal to 10 percent of the gross annual wages of the affected employees. The community payments would be used for redevelopment.[4] Under the proposed National Employment Priorities Act, if a business move is deemed "unjustified" by the secretary of labor, the business would be denied important tax benefits: the investment tax credit, accelerated depreciation allowances, the foreign tax credit, deferral of tax on income earned outside the United States, and deductions from taxable income of any expenses incurred in the move to the new location.[5]

Third, supporters of proposals for restricting business relocations advocate that government assistance be provided to people adversely affected by business movements. Under the proposed National Employment Priorities Act, the secretary of labor, with the advice of the National Employment Relocation Advisory Council,[6] would have been empowered to provide financial and technical assistance to (1)

---

[2] *National Employment Priorities Act of 1977*, p. 6.

[3] *Employment Relocation Assistanct Act*, pp. 2–3.

[4] State of Ohio, S. B. no. 337, p. 10.

[5] *National Employment Priorities Act of 1977*, pp. 33–35.

[6] The National Employment Relocation Advisory Council would consist of thirteen members: the secretaries of labor and commerce, the administrator of the Environmental Protection Agency, four members from the general public, three members from organized labor, and three members from the business community. The council would have authority to make whatever studies were needed to evaluate proposed business closings and transfers and the effectiveness of the council's decisions.

employees who lose their jobs because of business closings or transfers, (2) communities that suffer because of plant relocations, and (3) businesses that plan to close or move but may be able to stay in their present locations if assistance is made available.[7]

Government assistance to employees would take various forms, including cash payments, maintenance of health and pension benefits, relocation allowances, rental and mortgage supplements, retraining assistance, early retirement payments, food stamps, and distribution of surplus commodities. Federal grants would compensate communities for as much as 85 percent of any loss in tax revenues caused by closings and relocations, and loans would be provided "to communities or to private enterprise for the purpose of expanding existing job opportunities."[8] Assistance to business would be given in the form of technical advice, loans, and loan guarantees, but only "if the administrator determines that such assistance will prevent or alleviate the potential employment loss from such closing or transfer."[9] The legislation proposed in New Jersey and Ohio would have provided for community and employee assistance, but to a lesser extent than the federal proposal.

Fourth, under various proposals, firms would be required to give notice of their plans to move or close. The proposed National Employment Priorities Act in Congress and the Ohio bill would have required businesses to give a two-year notice.[10] The proposed Employment Relocation Assistance Act in New Jersey would have required only a one-year notice.[11] Exceptions, of course, could be made, but only if the firm could demonstrate that meeting the notice requirement is unreasonable. In short, the several proposals would effectively require that businesses with some minimum number of employees petition a state and/or federal government agency for the right to move and hand over to that agency the right to define what constitutes "adequate justification" for business movements and closings. Firms could be fined or penalized through the elimination of tax benefits if they did not comply with the decision of the government agency.

Finally, the federal proposal would have required that businesses offer their employees, to the extent possible, comparable employment at the new business location.[12]

---

[7] *National Employment Priorities Act of 1977*, pp. 6–7 and 20–33.

[8] Ibid., p. 26.

[9] Ibid., p. 7.

[10] Ibid., pp. 14–20; and State of Ohio, S. B. no. 337, p. 8.

[11] *Employment Relocation Assistance Act*, p. 4.

[12] *National Employment Priorities Act of 1977*, p. 35.

The Argument for Restrictions

In describing the changing regional structure of the U.S. economy, a leading business magazine has written: "The second war between the states will take the form of political and economic maneuver. But the conflict can nonetheless be bitter and divisive because it will be a struggle for income, jobs, people, and capital."[13] The author of the National Employment Priorities Act has given a reasonably clear indication of the way the political battle lines will be drawn, the economic basis for them, and the character of the ensuing debate. He has argued before his colleagues in the House:

> The legislation is based on the premise that such closings and transfers may cause irreparable harm—both economic and social—to workers, communities, and the Nation. . . . My own congressional district suffered the effects of the runaway plant in 1972 when the Garwood plant in Wayne moved and left 600 unemployed workers behind. . . . Mr. Speaker, the reason these firms are moving away is not economic necessity but economic greed. For instance, the Federal Mogul Co. in Detroit signed a contract in 1971 with the United Auto Workers and 6 months later announced it would be moving to Alabama. A spokesman for the company was quoted as saying they were moving "not because we are not making money in Detroit, but because we can make more money in Alabama."[14]

The author goes on to cite several other examples of the economic effects of business relocation decisions, including the "catastrophic problems" Hawaii has experienced because of the "runaway pineapple industry." He concludes that these types of problems "can be found in nearly every state in the country."[15]

The Design of the Study

The purpose of this study is to evaluate the issues raised by proposals to restrict business movements in a variety of ways. The premises undergirding the proposals and the claims of their supporters are analyzed in detail in Chapters 2 and 3. These claims are contrasted with data on the magnitude of recent changes in regional income. The overrid-

---

[13] "The Second War between the States," *Business Week*, May 17, 1976, p. 92.
[14] U.S. Congress, House, *Congressional Record*, 94th Cong., 1st sess., June 10, 1974, p. 18559.
[15] Ibid., p. 18560.

ing conclusion drawn in those chapters is that restrictions on business mobility are a solution to a nonexistent problem and that the political rhetoric behind the proposed legislation is at best misguided.

Chapter 4 explains how markets adjust to changes in economic forces between and among regions of a country. It recognizes that competitive markets, interrelated at the regional as well as the international level, form a social system designed to accommodate the changes in preferences and productivity of a people who are free to do what they find is in their best interest. Within this conceptual framework, I evaluate the long-run consequences of restrictions on business mobility.

Proposals to restrict business mobility are, no doubt, founded upon noble objectives as well as a strong sense of pragmatic politics. They may help alleviate the short-run economic hardship of some people who are laid off by plant closings or relocations, although ameliorative measures such as unemployment compensation are already in place, and little would be added by another program such as this. Advocates, most of whom are from the northern industrial states, may use the legislation to retard temporarily the economic development of southeastern and southwestern sunbelt states and thereby stabilize the economies of their own regions. If implemented, however, the proposed restrictions would have perverse long-run effects that would retard the economic development of both the South and the North. This study finds that restrictions would slow the growth of national income, reduce the rise in real wage rates, contribute to inflation, increase unemployment, and reduce the social mobility of workers—while at the same time reducing business profits and the efficiency of the U.S. economy.

Three conclusions of the study are worthy of special note. First, the per capita incomes in various regions of the country have for decades been converging on the U.S. average. The average per capita income in the country and in all regions has, however, been rising, in part as a result of the reallocation of resources among regions. The rising income is to be expected in free markets that allocate resources from less productive to more productive uses. Inasmuch as the convergence of regional incomes has brought us close to a long-run equilibrium, there will be much less movement of business and people among regions in the future. Restrictions are being proposed for a "problem" that is disappearing.

Second, data reveal that a minuscule percentage of all plant closings, 1.5 percent, are caused by relocation. The overwhelming majority of job losses in the North is due to the deaths of firms.

Those stark facts suggest that many of the economic problems of the North may be attributed to misguided public policies, not to wage and other attractions elsewhere.

Third, the economies of northern states are expanding; wage rates are rising; living conditions are improving. Many firms are leaving the North simply because they cannot keep up with the competition for labor and other resources from expanding sectors of the northern economies. To the extent this is true, movements of firms to other regions from the North reflect the improving (not worsening) economic conditions of the North. Restrictions on business movements will simply retard the economic expansion of the North.

Government restrictions on business movements raise once again the specter of "1984," the creation of another government bureaucracy, and another layer of administrative law. Given the persistence of supporters of these proposals, the growing support for them, the likely increase in the political attractiveness of relocation restrictions in any future downturn in the business cycle, and the existence of similar restrictions in several European countries, careful examination of the premises underlying the proposals is timely. We ought to know what consequences to anticipate from such proposals and take them into consideration in arriving at conclusions about the appropriate role of government in relocation decisions.

2

The Snowbelt versus the Sunbelt

The campaign for the governmental restriction of business mobility has been initiated with all the rhetoric of war. Phrases like "second war between the states," "counterattacks," and "fierce and ruinous state warfare" pepper the popular accounts of changes in the regional structure of the U.S. economy. The rhetoric is useful to proponents of relocation rules and to news reporters because it grabs the reader's attention, makes economic conditions in regions which are declining in a *relative* sense appear desperate in an absolute sense, and encourages the view that drastic political action is not only desirable but unavoidable. Here, the case for relocation rules is presented issue by issue, and the rhetoric of the case is set in contrast with the facts of regional change.

The following analysis for the most part refers to regions and subdivisions of the country as defined in Figure 1. Because much of the debate on relocation rules and regional adjustments is couched in terms of the North versus the South or the snowbelt versus the sunbelt, however, attention will focus on the northern industrial tier, made up of states in the Northeast and the East North Central regions, and on the South, composed of the South Atlantic, East South Central, and West South Central states.

Population Shifts

Advocates of relocation restrictions point to relative population growth rates as barometers of the economic health of different regions, as symptoms of the underlying causes of business migration, and as indicators of the consequences of unrestrained business movements. News accounts of regional adjustments give the impression that a decline in population growth *rates* should be construed as a decline

8

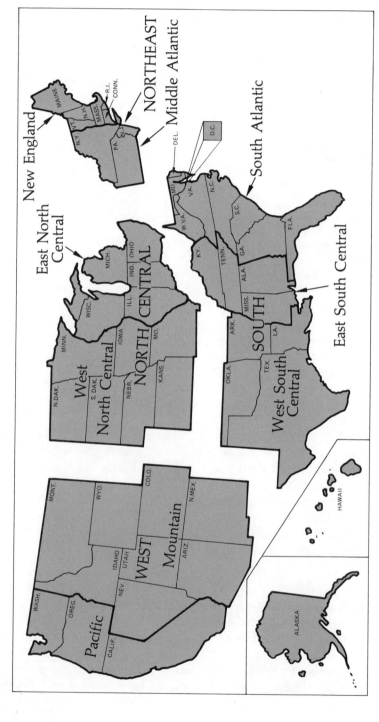

FIGURE 1

REGIONS AND DIVISIONS OF THE UNITED STATES

NOTE: Pacific division includes Alaska and Hawaii.

in population *levels* and that something is fundamentally wrong with economic and political institutions when population growth rates among regions differ.

In its account of "The Second War between the States," *Business Week* writes, "As long as the migration of industry and population was gradual from what was a relatively rich Northeast to what was a relatively impoverished South and Southwest, it [migration] helped to unify the country. But within the last five years the process has burst beyond the bounds that can be accommodated by existing political institutions." The magazine goes on to point out that

> less than three years ago [in 1973], the Commerce Dept.'s Bureau of Economic Analysis published projections for 1980 and 1990 of the population, personal income, and employment in each of the 50 states. By last year [1975] nine growth states—Arkansas, Louisiana, Mississippi, South Carolina, Arizona, Texas, Utah, Alaska, and Hawaii—had already exceeded their 1980 projections in population, and one state— New Mexico—had already surpassed the 1990 figure. By the same token, the shortfall in slower-growing regions has been enormous.

The point is made that New York lost more than 100,000 people when it was expected to gain more than a million, and "Pennsylvania, slated to gain nearly 800,000 during the 1970s, has increased its population by barely 30,000 thus far." The publication goes on to suggest that the population growth of the South and Southwest has been "meteoric" because of immigration of people from the Northeast.[1]

Casual perusal of Figure 2, which portrays the population growth rates of each state, shows that the slower growing states are in the Northeast and North Central regions of the country. New York and Pennsylvania actually had decreases in population during the 1970–1977 period, while the populations of most southern and western states grew by more than 6 percent. Table 1 shows that the population growth rates of southern and western states have exceeded those of the northern industrial tier for nearly three decades, but the population growth rates of *all* regions have been declining since the 1950s. The population growth rate of the North Central region declined from 16.1 percent in the 1950s to 9.6 percent in the 1960s; that of the West declined from nearly 39 percent in the 1950s to 24 percent in the 1960s. Nevertheless, the population of all major regions has increased consistently over the period covered by the table.

---

[1] "The Second War between the States," *Business Week*, May 17, 1976, p. 92.

10

FIGURE 2

PERCENTAGE CHANGE IN POPULATION BY STATE, 1970–1977

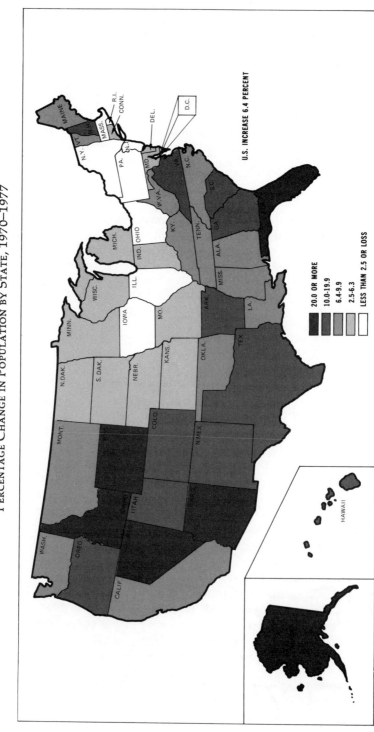

U.S. INCREASE 6.4 PERCENT

20.0 OR MORE
10.0–19.9
6.4–9.9
2.5–6.3
LESS THAN 2.5 OR LOSS

SOURCE: U.S. Bureau of the Census, *Current Population Reports*, Series P-20, no. 324, "Population Profile of the United States: 1977" (April 1978), p. 30 and

TABLE 1
REGIONAL POPULATION GROWTH PATTERNS, 1950–1977
(thousands)

Region and Division	1950	1960	1970	1977	Percentage Change 1950–1960	Percentage Change 1960–1970	Percentage Change 1970–1977
Northeast	39,478	44,678	49,061	49,280	13.2	9.8	0.4
New England	9,314	10,509	11,847	12,242	12.8	12.7	3.3
Middle Atlantic	30,164	34,168	37,213	37,038	13.3	8.9	−0.4
North Central	44,461	51,619	56,593	57,941	16.1	9.6	2.3
East North Central	30,399	36,225	40,266	41,057	19.2	11.2	2.0
West North Central	14,061	15,394	16,328	16,884	9.5	6.1	3.4
South	47,197	54,973	62,812	69,849	16.4	14.3	11.2
South Atlantic	21,182	25,972	30,679	34,305	22.6	18.1	11.8
East South Central	11,477	12,050	12,808	13,837	5.0	6.3	8.0
West South Central	14,538	16,951	19,325	21,707	16.6	14.0	12.3
West	20,190	28,053	34,838	39,263	38.9	24.2	12.7
Mountain	5,075	6,855	8,290	10,031	35.1	20.9	21.0
Pacific	15,115	21,198	26,549	29,232	40.2	25.2	10.1
U.S. total	151,326	179,323	203,304	216,332	18.5	13.4	6.4

NOTE: Because of rounding, sums of individual items may not equal totals.
SOURCE: George Sternlieb and James W. Hughes, *Current Population Trends in the United States* (New Brunswick, N.J.: Center for Urban Policy Research, 1978), p. 61; based on U.S. census figures for 1950, 1960, and 1970; and U.S. Bureau of the Census, *Current Population Reports*, Series P-25, no. 640, "Estimates of the Population of States with Components of Change: 1970 to 1975" (November 1976).

TABLE 2

Region	Population		Natural Increase		Net Migration	
	1970–1976	1960–1970	1970–1976	1960–1970	1970–1976	1960–1970
United States	0.9	1.3	0.7	1.1	0.2	0.2
Northeast	0.1	0.9	0.4	0.9	−0.3	0.1
North Central	0.3	0.9	0.6	1.0	−0.3	−0.1
South	1.5	1.3	0.8	1.2	0.7	0.2
West	1.6	2.2	0.8	1.3	0.8	1.0

Source: U.S. Bureau of the Census, *Current Population Reports*, Series P-20, no. 324, "Population Profile of the United States: 1977" (April 1978), table 17.

Table 2 provides more detailed information on regional population growth rates. It shows that the average annual increase in the U.S. population was 0.9 percent between 1970 and 1976, down from an average annual increase of 1.3 percent from 1960 to 1970. The table also indicates that the average annual increase in the South and West was substantially higher than in the Northeast and North Central states. In the 1970–1976 period, only the South had an average annual population growth rate greater than that of the 1960–1970 period.

Table 2 breaks down the average annual population growth rate figures into two major components: natural increases (births minus deaths) and growth caused by in-migration (minus out-migration). In 1970–1976, for example, the Northeast had an average yearly growth rate of 0.1 percent with a natural rate of increase of 0.4 percent offset by a net migration of −0.3 percent. People moved into the area from other regions, but on balance more people moved out than moved in. Contrary to news accounts, the net migration of people from the North can hardly be characterized as "meteoric" by any stretch of the imagination. Similarly, the North Central region had an average annual natural population increase of 0.6 percent, but it lost people at the rate of −0.3 percent a year. The resulting average yearly increase in the population of the North Central region was, therefore, 0.3 percent.

The South, on the other hand, had a 1.5 percent average annual population increase because of a 0.8 percent natural increase and a

0.7 percent net migration. The population of the West grew slightly more rapidly, at an average annual rate of 1.6 percent because of a natural increase of 0.8 and a net migration of 0.8 percent.

The data in Table 2 are useful for another purpose: they show that the drop in the population growth rate of the Northeast was caused as much by a decrease in natural factors as by migration. The annual natural rate of population growth in the Northeast dropped by more than 55 percent, from 0.9 to 0.4, in the 1970–1976 period. In short, less than half the drop in the average annual growth rate of population in the Northeast from 1970 to 1976 can be attributed to out-migration. The growth in the use of contraception and in the number of abortions and the trend toward smaller families, reflecting changes in social values, had a greater role in the decrease in northern population growth than did business relocations. In addition, a significant number of people move South, not because their jobs are being relocated there, but because they choose a warmer climate for a retirement home or they are attracted by the increasing employment opportunities in the South as new firms open and old firms expand.

The South and West also experienced substantial decreases in the natural rates of population growth, but the decreases were not nearly as dramatic as those in the North. Consequently, even without migration from the North to the South and the West, there would have been a substantial decrease in the rate of population growth in the North in relation to that of the South. Furthermore, the overall population growth of the South in the first half of the 1970s was significantly affected by the nearly 25 percent population growth of one state, Florida. Much of that growth came not from the movement of industry, but from the movement of retired people seeking Florida's sunshine.

In making the case for restrictions on business mobility, the proponents have attempted to garner political support within their region by making the issue one of "us" against "them," much as the case for tariffs is made on the basis of domestic jobs versus foreign jobs. However, the division of the country into geographical regions, like those drawn in Figure 1, is largely artificial. Such divisions have no economic meaning to a business interested in maximizing profits or to a person who seeks to find the most suitable place to live, given his or her preferences. Because distance influences the cost of moves and the cost of moves determines how many people move and how far they move, more migration occurs within a region than among regions. This is especially true when accents, relatives, and customs affect the willingness of people to move. Indeed, Table 3 shows that

13

TABLE 3

GEOGRAPHICAL MOBILITY, MARCH 1975–MARCH 1977, OF PERSONS TWO YEARS OLD AND OVER, BY REGION OF RESIDENCE IN 1977
(thousands)

Residence in 1977	United States	North-east	North Central	South	West
Population two years old and over	206,419	47,329	55,611	66,256	37,224
Same house	149,789	37,862	41,262	46,939	23,727
Different house in					
United States	54,620	9,087	13,927	18,771	12,835
Same county	33,258	5,531	8,797	10,985	7,945
Different county	21,362	3,556	5,131	7,786	4,889
Same State	11,417	2,292	3,014	3,893	2,217
Different State	9,946	1,263	2,117	3,893	2,672
Northeast	1,878	595	249	699	335
North Central	2,479	181	921	762	615
South	3,431	329	581	1,961	560
West	2,157	158	367	471	1,162
Abroad	2,010	380	422	546	662

SOURCE: U.S. Bureau of the Census, *Current Population Reports*, Series P-20, no. 320, "Geographical Mobility: March 1975 to March 1977" (February 1978), table 2.

more than 50 percent of the people who moved between 1975 and 1977 stayed within the same county. In the Northeast, only 36 percent of those who moved to a different county ended up in a different state. Many of these people, no doubt, moved merely a few miles, from one side of a state boundary to the other. Of the nearly 1.3 million northeasterners who moved to another state between 1975 and 1977, 47 percent stayed in the Northeast; only 26 percent moved to the South, and only 12 percent moved to the West.

As can be seen in Table 3, in all regions most people who move stay within the region. An important conclusion can be drawn: If business relocation rules are seen as a means of restricting people's migration, they will restrict migration within regions as much as or more than among regions. If business relocation rules are designed to retard the economic development of the South and West by restricting the migration of people and jobs, they will also restrict the economic development of the Northeast and the North Central. It is a gross distortion of the facts to develop the case for business relocation rules as one in which one region is pitted against another.

News accounts of migration between the North and South leave the impression that the Northeast and North Central regions are being adversely affected not only by the number of people who are moving South, but also by the demographic characteristics of the in- and out-migration flows. For example, one report states that

> during the 1960s the major movements between the North and South were of middle-class whites to the South and low-income blacks to the North. These flows were almost equal in size, with the South attaining only a small net increase. Since 1970, however, burgeoning economic opportunity—especially in the South and Southwest but also in the Plains states—greatly retarded the outflow and accelerated the inflow.[2]

Tables 4 and 5 do not bear out this picture, however. For instance, the number of unemployed male workers (23,000) who moved from the Northeast to the South was substantially greater than the number of unemployed male workers (14,000) who moved from the South to the Northeast in the 1975–1977 period. Virtually the same thing can be said about the number of unemployed females who moved from the Northeast to the South and from the South to the Northeast. Similarly, the Northeast exported more unemployed workers to the West than it imported from the West. Other observations are equally revealing (Table 6): First, far more people below the poverty line (133,000) migrated from the Northeast to the South than from the South to the Northeast (39,000). Second, while more people with one or more years of college migrated from the Northeast to the South (151,000) than from the South to the Northeast (102,000), those with some college education were a significantly greater proportion of the southern migrants to the North (56.3 percent) than of the northern migrants to the South (40.3 percent). Third, although Tables 4 and 5 reveal that more professional workers moved from the Northeast to the South than from the South to the Northeast, this is true for almost all other categories of workers listed and may be expected when more people are moving out of the Northeast than are moving in. On a percentage basis, it is not clear that the South or West is getting from the North a disproportionate number of highly trained people. The South is taking in more highly trained people than it is sending out; but by the same token, it is taking in more unemployed people than it is sending out. Finally, over 50 percent more blacks

---

[2] Ibid.

TABLE 4

MALE INTERREGIONAL MIGRANTS, BY EMPLOYMENT STATUS AND OCCUPATION, 1975–1977

(thousands)

Employment Status and Occupation	From Northeast to:			From North Central to:			From South to:			From West to:		
	North Central	South	West	North-east	South	West	North-east	North Central	West	North-east	North Central	South
Total male migrants, 16 to 64 years old	95	200	130	72	278	230	125	221	208	71	162	174
Civilian labor force	75	155	106	65	201	185	106	183	142	55	128	108
Employed workers	70	132	79	57	182	158	92	145	115	46	107	97
Professional, technical	29	40	26	26	31	34	30	32	26	11	26	25
Managers and administrators, except farm	13	23	9	12	35	27	15	24	14	7	11	13
Sales	—	7	6	7	20	10	3	9	8	3	4	3
Clerical and kindred	5	6	5	3	13	9	—	3	11	5	—	4
Crafts and kindred	10	24	18	5	27	33	18	34	16	4	26	27
Operators, except transport equipment	7	10	4	2	22	9	9	22	15	4	11	9
Transport equipment	—	1	4	—	15	8	6	2	4	3	7	5
Laborers, except farm	2	15	1	—	9	9	6	11	9	—	14	6
Farm	—	—	—	2	4	6	2	3	3	—	—	1
Service	4	5	5	1	4	13	5	6	8	8	9	4
Unemployed	5	23	27	8	19	27	14	37	27	9	21	11
Armed forces	9	24	12	4	32	19	6	14	36	9	18	30
Not in labor force	11	20	12	4	46	26	13	24	30	6	16	36

SOURCE: U.S. Bureau of the Census, *Current Population Reports*, tables 41 and 42.

TABLE 5

Female Interregional Migrants, by Employment Status and Occupation, 1975–1977
(thousands)

Employment Status and Occupation	From Northeast to:			From North Central to:			From South to:			From West to:		
	North Central	South	West	North-east	South	West	North-east	North Central	West	North-east	North Central	South
Total female migrants, 16 to 64 years old	108	243	117	70	249	207	112	186	178	51	122	152
Civilian labor force	51	107	66	50	122	122	61	96	98	36	73	34
Employed workers	47	86	55	44	100	103	48	89	84	29	63	47
Professional, technical	18	25	7	10	17	17	8	24	8	10	15	11
Managers and administrators, except farm	—	3	2	2	5	4	5	1	6	2	—	6
Sales	4	9	10	2	8	7	4	5	4	1	10	1
Clerical and kindred	15	22	15	21	30	36	11	31	45	10	20	15
Crafts and kindred	—	—	2	—	2	—	2	2	—	—	—	—
Operators, except transport equipment	—	12	2	—	13	8	5	9	8	3	4	3
Transport equipment	—	—	—	—	—	—	2	—	—	—	—	1
Laborers, except farm	—	—	3	—	3	1	—	—	—	—	—	—
Farm	—	—	—	—	—	—	—	—	—	—	—	—
Service	10	14	14	9	22	29	12	18	12	3	13	10
Unemployed	4	21	11	6	22	19	12	6	14	6	11	7
Not in labor force	57	136	51	20	127	85	51	90	80	15	49	98

SOURCE: U.S. Bureau of the Census, *Current Population Reports*, tables 41 and 42.

17

TABLE 6

Total Interregional Migrants, by Education, Income Level, and Race, 1975–1977
(thousands)

Characteristic	From Northeast to:			From North Central to:			From South to:			From West to:		
	North Central	South	West	North-east	South	West	North-east	North Central	West	North-east	North Central	South
Years of school completed												
Total, 25 years old and over	128	374	162	101	412	309	181	261	259	259	178	238
Elementary: 0 to 8 years	2	60	21	3	59	20	10	30	25	12	15	24
High School												
1–3 years	9	45	14	5	56	46	15	32	31	11	14	22
4 years	30	118	36	25	136	97	55	79	87	25	56	86
College												
1–3 years	20	55	37	15	66	52	36	41	55	9	23	45
4 years	31	60	24	19	52	61	33	44	31	12	35	27
5 years or more	36	36	30	34	43	32	33	35	30	11	35	34
Relative income level												
Total, 2 years old and over	249	699	335	181	762	615	329	581	560	158	367	471
Above poverty level	217	567	265	173	639	518	290	472	524	141	331	419
Below poverty level	32	133	70	8	123	97	39	108	36	17	36	54
Race												
Total, 2 years old and over	249	894	335	181	762	615	329	581	560	158	367	471
White, 2 years old and over	218	578	305	167	692	584	297	495	483	154	353	441
Black, 2 years old and over	22	104	21	7	64	21	33	78	55	3	6	15

Source: U.S. Bureau of the Census, *Current Population Reports*, tables 41 and 42.

migrated from the Northeast and North Central regions to the South than went from the South to the Northeast and North Central regions.

In summary, there has been a significant change in the relative population growth rate of the North, but it is one that has been under way for three decades. The relatively modest immigration of people into the North in the 1960s has changed to a relatively modest out-migration of people from the North to other parts of the country. But, as C. L. Jusenius and L. C. Ledebur have commented in a report on the economic myths of southern growth,

> the extent to which it represents a new long-run trend—rather than a cyclical response to the recent severe economic recession—is unclear. Workers, reacting to unemployment in highly industrial areas, may be returning *temporarily* to their place of origin where a network of friends and relatives as well as marginal employment opportunities exist. Such a phenomenon is not without historical precedent: it occurred extensively during the Great Depression.

Jusenius and Ledebur conclude that "At this point the evidence is inconclusive. . . . This uncertainty argues for, at least, a reasonable amount of caution in the creation of public policy based on the current migration experience."[3]

Per Capita Income Changes

Reports on industry relocation give the impression that if the North is not now worse off economically than the South and Southwest, it is rapidly approaching the South's lower standard of living because of relocations. Edward Kelly, in *Industrial Exodus*, a position paper of the Conference for Alternative State and Local Public Policies that endorses the desirability of relocation restrictions, writes, "As the manufacturing base of the [northern] economy declines, so does the tax base. There are fewer taxable industrial locations and fewer people capable of paying taxes."[4] Further, the *National Journal* reports:

> In general, those states in the most favorable balance of payments position [in terms of taxes paid and government benefits received] with Washington were the ones in the

[3] C. L. Jusenius and L. C. Ledebur, *A Myth in the Making: The Southern Economic Challenge and Northern Economic Decline* (Washington, D.C.: Department of Commerce, Economic Development Administration, November 1976), p. 3.

[4] Edward Kelly, *Industrial Exodus: Public Strategies for Control of Runaway Plants* (Washington, D.C.: Conference for Alternative State and Local Public Policies, October 1977), pp. 7–8.

FIGURE 3
PER CAPITA PERSONAL INCOME, 1977

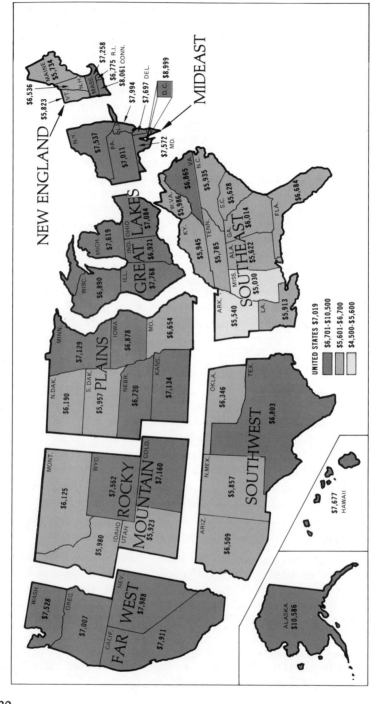

UNITED STATES $7,019

$6,701-$10,500
$5,601-$6,700
$4,500-$5,600

SOURCE: *Survey of Current Business*, August 1978.

South and West that have been experiencing the heaviest population gains, the least unemployment and the strongest gains in per capita income. . . . On the other hand, the balance of payments situation generally is adverse in the Northeast and Midwest, where population is declining, where unemployment is the most severe, where relative personal income is falling and where the heaviest state and local tax burdens are imposed.[5]

Contrary to the impression given by these accounts of the relative welfare of residents in the North and South, Figure 3 clearly reveals that most lower income states are in the South and Southwest. Per capita personal income in 1977 was much higher in the Northeast, North Central, and Far West than in the Southeast and Southwest. As shown in the far right-hand column of Table 7, only the states of Maine, Vermont, and North Dakota in the industrial snowbelt had per capita income levels which fall below the 1977 national average by more than six percentage points. The Mideast, Great Lakes, and New England divisions of the country had 1977 per capita income levels which were 106, 105, and 102 percent of the national average while the Southeast and Southwest regions had average income levels which were 86 and 95 percent of the national average.

In evaluating the arguments for business relocation rules, an elementary but important point must be kept in mind: the per capita income levels of *all* regions of the country rose during the 1970s, even after adjustments are made for the effects of inflation. Since the populations of all regions grew during the period, it follows that total regional incomes also grew. Therefore, although regional tax bases may not have grown as much as desired, the tax bases of all regions have still grown. This generality, however, may not hold for individual states and subdivisions of states.

If there is any basis for concern over the economic health of the North, it must be in terms of the relative income levels of northern states. As clearly shown in Figure 4, the per capita personal income of the Mideast (Delaware, District of Columbia, Maryland, New Jersey, New York, and Pennsylvania) has been on a steady decline relative to the Southeast (Alabama, Arkansas, Florida, Georgia, Kentucky, Louisiana, Mississippi, North and South Carolina, Tennessee, Virginia, and West Virginia) since 1929. In 1929 the per capita disposable income of the Mideast was more than 159 percent higher than the per capita disposable income in the Southeast. In 1977 the per capita

---

[5] "Federal Spending: The North's Loss Is the Sunbelt's Gain," *National Journal,* June 26, 1976, p. 878.

FIGURE 4
Index of Regional per Capita Disposable Income
(U.S. Average = 100)

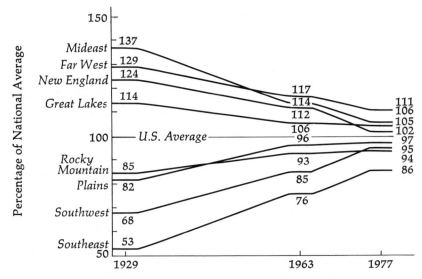

Source: Yale Brozen, Department of Economics, University of Chicago (personal calculations).

income of the Mideast was only 23 percent greater than that of the Southeast.

Historically, the trend of the per capita income of the New England and Great Lakes divisions relative to the per capita income of the Southeast has also declined steadily. Since the cost of living has generally risen slightly faster in the South than in the northern industrial tier, the convergence of per capita income of the regions in terms of real purchasing power has been slightly less pronounced than Figure 4 suggests. It is still clear, however, that northern industrial states have on average a substantially higher standard of living as measured by income figures. That explains in large measure why more people have not moved South. Furthermore, it is clear from Figure 4 that proponents of restrictions have proposed a solution to a problem—the migration of industry—which has already been largely resolved through normal market forces. Given the convergence in regional standards of living, the long-term movement of industry is likely to be less dramatic in the future than it has been in the past.

The movement of industry and people South does not mean that the North is therefore made worse off or that the *growth* in the standard of living in the North has been retarded. Indeed, the con-

22

TABLE 7

PER CAPITA PERSONAL INCOME, BY REGION AND STATE, 1971–1977
(dollars)

Region and State	1971	1972	1973	1974	1975	1976	1977	Percentage of National Average	
								1971	1977
United States	4,132	4,493	4,980	5,428	5,861	6,403	7,019	100	100
New England	4,416	4,747	5,764	5,635	6,930	6,568	7,183	107	102
Connecticut	4,998	5,353	5,869	6,391	6,799	7,313	8,061	121	115
Maine	3,396	3,636	4,085	4,493	4,766	5,367	5,734	82	82
Massachusetts	4,469	4,816	5,198	5,666	6,077	6,533	7,258	108	103
New Hampshire	3,876	4,193	4,604	5,022	5,417	5,974	6,536	94	93
Rhode Island	4,105	4,433	4,779	5,287	5,709	6,187	6,775	99	97
Vermont	3,630	3,906	4,225	4,580	4,924	5,414	5,823	88	83
Mideast	4,635	4,985	5,415	5,928	6,330	6,878	7,479	112	106
Delaware	4,732	5,085	5,640	6,078	6,547	7,107	7,697	111	110
District of Columbia	5,064	5,523	5,952	6,595	7,262	8,120	8,999	124	128
Maryland	4,539	4,949	5,460	5,951	6,403	6,995	7,570	109	108
New Jersey	4,967	5,326	5,807	6,326	6,794	7,314	7,994	120	114
New York	4,859	5,178	5,561	6,076	6,519	6,929	7,537	118	107
Pennsylvania	4,086	4,451	4,890	5,402	5,841	6,402	7,011	99	100
Great Lakes	4,318	4,679	5,211	5,644	6,047	6,688	7,347	105	105
Illinois	4,744	5,075	5,666	6,215	6,735	7,322	7,768	115	111
Indiana	3,974	4,314	4,909	5,225	5,609	6,259	6,921	90	99

(Table continues on next page.)

TABLE 7 (CONTINUED)

Region and State	1971	1972	1973	1974	1975	1976	1977	Percentage of National Average 1971	Percentage of National Average 1977
Michigan	4,371	4,804	5,340	5,670	5,991	6,765	7,619	106	109
Ohio	4,153	4,512	4,973	5,433	5,778	6,400	7,084	101	101
Wisconsin	3,945	4,266	4,747	5,182	5,616	6,136	6,890	95	98
Plains	3,878	4,274	5,037	5,267	5,719	6,110	6,830	94	97
Iowa	3,788	4,218	5,166	5,327	5,894	6,172	6,878	92	98
Kansas	4,017	4,470	5,149	5,505	5,958	6,507	7,134	97	102
Minnesota	3,999	4,358	5,115	5,422	5,779	6,237	7,129	97	102
Missouri	3,887	4,185	4,689	5,007	5,476	5,968	6,654	94	95
Nebraska	3,904	4,364	5,127	5,196	5,882	6,112	6,720	94	96
North Dakota	3,448	4,235	6,064	5,879	5,888	5,773	6,190	84	88
South Dakota	3,371	3,847	4,948	4,753	5,009	5,097	5,957	82	85
Southeast	3,458	3,829	4,278	4,689	5,028	5,536	6,055	84	86
Alabama	3,131	3,439	3,852	4,233	4,635	5,138	5,622	76	80
Arkansas	2,999	3,302	3,829	4,271	4,510	4,923	5,540	73	79
Florida	4,007	4,461	4,973	5,338	5,631	6,105	6,684	97	95
Georgia	3,550	3,953	4,391	4,755	5,029	5,531	6,014	86	86
Kentucky	3,278	3,613	4,021	4,520	4,887	5,414	5,945	79	85
Louisiana	3,227	3,493	3,899	4,373	4,803	5,337	5,913	78	84
Mississippi	2,770	3,094	3,460	3,781	4,047	4,543	5,030	67	72
North Carolina	3,431	3,810	4,251	4,624	4,940	5,478	5,935	83	85
South Carolina	3,169	3,519	3,945	4,405	4,665	5,197	5,628	77	80
Tennessee	3,333	3,696	4,149	4,506	4,804	5,305	5,785	81	82

Virginia	3,973	4,386	4,851	5,337	5,772	6,314	6,865	97	98
West Virginia	3,287	3,612	3,981	4,425	4,962	5,476	5,986	79	85
Southwest	3,669	4,023	4,517	4,979	5,469	6,017	6,642	89	95
Arizona	3,928	4,319	4,744	5,123	5,391	5,944	6,509	95	93
New Mexico	3,265	3,596	3,936	4,328	4,843	5,298	5,857	79	83
Oklahoma	3,509	3,841	4,371	4,822	5,280	5,707	6,346	85	90
Texas	3,700	4,053	4,564	5,048	5,584	6,166	6,803	90	97
Rocky Mountain	3,794	4,189	4,734	5,157	5,571	6,094	6,618	92	94
Colorado	4,167	4,540	5,046	5,495	5,987	6,527	7,160	101	102
Idaho	3,434	3,872	4,482	5,028	5,179	5,678	5,980	83	85
Montana	3,503	4,013	4,760	4,976	5,388	5,669	6,125	85	87
Utah	3,427	3,719	4,100	4,462	4,900	5,422	5,923	83	84
Wyoming	3,847	4,352	5,120	5,653	6,123	6,764	7,562	93	108
Far West	4,530	4,908	5,353	5,910	6,474	7,104	7,788	110	111
California	4,647	5,022	5,444	6,015	6,575	7,219	7,911	113	113
Nevada	4,825	5,167	5,698	6,063	6,625	7,198	7,988	117	114
Oregon	3,944	4,338	4,829	5,312	5,769	6,368	7,007	95	100
Washington	4,161	4,545	5,089	5,647	6,298	6,878	7,528	101	107
Alaska	4,939	5,234	6,066	7,137	9,636	10,124	10,580	120	151
Hawaii	4,785	5,078	5,564	6,134	6,708	7,183	7,677	116	109

SOURCE: *Survey of Current Business*, August 1978, p. 16.

verse may be reasonably argued: movements of people and industry have contributed to the growth in the standard of living in the North. By moving South, where production costs are lower, industries are able to provide goods and services to northern markets at lower prices than they would have been able to provide if they had stayed in the North.

The greater production which can result at lower costs contributes to greater national income and, because the prices of goods and services are lower, to an increase in the purchasing power of workers' incomes, including the incomes of workers in the North. Also, incomes in the North have increased because it changed its industrial composition to specialize in the industries where it had a comparative advantage. The industries that declined in the North were the low-wage industries while those that grew were the high-wage industries. If industry had not moved South, real incomes in the North would have risen less rapidly than they have. Granted, when a company pulls up stakes and moves, some people may be left behind without jobs. As shown in a later section of this chapter, however, the loss in income suffered by persons thus unemployed can be more than compensated for by expanding employment in other, higher wage areas of the regional economy and by the beneficial effects of reduced production costs and lower prices of goods and services. The result is some redistribution of income, but still higher per capita income.

Furthermore, job losses because of business relocations are often exaggerated. As an example, the shutdown of a major steel plant in Youngstown, Ohio, in 1977 eliminated 5,000 industrial jobs in the area, but the unemployment rate by mid-1978 was only 7.5 percent, lower than a year earlier when it was 8.4 percent. Many of those unemployed by the shutdown of the steel plant got other jobs; others chose to remain unemployed because of unemployment compensation and trade adjustment assistance. More will be said on this and related points in Chapter 3.

Federal Tax and Expenditure Policies

"Federal tax and spending policies are causing a *massive* flow of wealth from the Northeast and Midwest to the fast growing Southern and Western regions of the nation, according to a *National Journal* survey of financial relationships between the states and federal government." After this description of the federal government's contribution to the relatively higher growth rate of the South, the *National Journal* pointed out that in fiscal 1975 the five Great Lakes states had a "balance of payments deficit" with the federal government of $18.6 billion. Though they paid out $62.2 billion in federal taxes, they received only $43.6 billion in federal outlays. Similarly, the Mid-Atlantic states sent $10 billion more in taxes to Washington than they received in return. On the other hand, the South and West had a "balance of payments surplus" with Washington of $11.5 billion and $10.6 billion, respectively.[6]

The *National Journal* did not say how much of the income on which taxes were paid was actually earned in these regions. Since a disproportionate share of the country's major corporations have their home offices in the Northeast and Midwest, a part of the taxes paid there was from income earned outside the regions. Commenting on the accidental way in which "inequities" can arise from federal tax collections and disbursements, the *Journal* stated that "Florida gets more than its share of social security outlays because many elderly persons live there."[7] One must wonder why Florida should not get a disproportionate share of the social security benefits if a disproportionate share of the elderly live there.

Table 8 shows that for fiscal year 1975, states in the northern industrial tier paid more per capita in taxes than they received in the form of government outlays. The opposite was true of the sunbelt. Per capita, the northern states paid approximately 27 percent more in taxes ($1,560) than they received in expenditures ($1,224), whereas the per capita taxes of southern states were only 88 percent of their per person federal receipts. As Jusenius and Ledebur explain, however,

> one of the functions of fiscal policy is to redistribute income among groups according to goals determined by society. One of the redistributive goals, however well met, has been to close the gap between "the rich" and "the poor." In part, the Federal Government has attempted to meet this goal through the Federal income tax system: taxpayers with higher income levels also pay relatively higher proportions of their incomes in taxes. On the expenditure side, public policy has been directed toward raising the real income of the lowest socioeconomic groups.[8]

As shown in the previous section, the per capita income in the South is lower than in the North.

Table 8 also gives the per capita income levels of the sunbelt

---

[6] Ibid., emphasis added in quotation.

[7] Ibid.

[8] Jusenius and Ledebur, *A Myth in the Making*, p. 28.

TABLE 8

FEDERAL SPENDING, FEDERAL TAXES, AND PERSONAL INCOME PER CAPITA, FISCAL YEAR 1975
(dollars)

Region and State	Federal Spending per Person	Federal Taxes per Person	Per Capita Personal Income	Federal Taxes as a Percentage of Income
Sunbelt	1,356	1,188	5,176	23.0
South Atlantic	1,392	1,249	5,288	23.6
Florida	1,379	1,378	5,638	24.4
Georgia	1,402	1,217	5,086	23.9
North Carolina	1,124	1,145	4,952	23.1
South Carolina	1,240	1,041	4,618	22.5
Virginia	1,809	1,355	5,785	23.4
West Virginia	1,318	1,091	4,918	22.2
East South Central	1,377	1,060	4,676	22.7
Alabama	1,374	1,026	4,643	22.1
Kentucky	1,327	1,094	4,871	22.5
Mississippi	1,599	908	4,052	22.4
Tennessee	1,296	1,147	4,895	23.4
West South Central	1,295	1,187	5,347	22.2
Arkansas	1,202	907	4,620	19.6
Louisiana	1,236	1,064	4,904	21.7
Oklahoma	1,443	1,181	5,250	22.5
Texas	1,296	1,264	5,631	22.5

and northern industrial tier and the percentage of income paid in taxes. It shows that in 1975 the northern states paid, on average, slightly higher tax rates than states in the South. As a percentage of income, the average tax rate in the sunbelt was 23.0 and in the northern industrial tier, 24.9. Since the per capita income in the North was approximately 21 percent higher than in the South, and the U.S. tax rate system is progressive, the slightly higher rate of taxation in the North is to be expected, a point that Jusenius and Ledebur stress in their analysis of the same data.[9]

[9] With additional data computed by the *National Journal*, Jusenius and Ledebur point out that per person expenditures on defense contracts were about the same in the North ($167) as in the South ($161). However, since a disproportionate share of defense bases are located in the South, per person defense salaries were much greater in the South ($188) than in the North ($54). Per person expenditures on highway and sewer systems, welfare programs, and retirement programs combined were fairly similar in the North ($548) and South ($560). (Ibid., pp. 30–32.)

TABLE 8 (CONTINUED)

Region and State	Federal Spending per Person	Federal Taxes per Person	Per Capita Personal Income	Federal Taxes as a Percentage of Income
Northern industrial tier	1,224	1,560	6,265	24.9
New England	1,510	1,611	6,358	25.3
Connecticut	1,663	1,800	6,973	25.8
Massachusetts	1,456	1,535	6,114	25.1
Rhode Island	1,342	1,457	5,841	24.9
East North Central	1,064	1,518	6,121	24.8
Illinois	1,230	1,704	6,789	25.1
Indiana	1,027	1,441	5,653	25.0
Michigan	996	1,539	6,173	24.9
Ohio	1,010	1,441	5,810	24.8
Wisconsin	996	1,331	5,669	23.5
Middle Atlantic	1,325	1,594	6,398	24.9
New Jersey	1,154	1,760	6,722	26.2
New York	1,449	1,636	6,564	24.9
Pennsylvania	1,241	1,426	5,943	24.0
National Average	1,412	1,412	5,902	23.9

SOURCES: "Federal Spending: The North's Loss Is the Sunbelt's Gain," *National Journal*, June 26, 1976, p. 881; and C. L. Jusenius and L. C. Ledebur, *A Myth in the Making: The Southern Economic Challenge and Northern Economic Decline* (Washington, D.C.: Department of Commerce, Economic Development Administration, November 1976).

It is important to note that the Federal Government spent *less* per person in both regions than in the Nation as a whole. While the Southern states are among the poorest in the country, they received less than the national average in per capita Federal Government expenditures. . . . In spite of the Federal Government's higher per capita spending in the South, these states still have, on average, a lower per capita personal income than the Northern states. Without this current flow of monies to the South, the income disparity between the two regions would be even greater.[10]

---

[10] Ibid., p. 28.

The higher marginal tax rates paid by residents in the northern industrial tier very likely contribute to production inefficiency and increase, albeit slightly, the competitive advantage of poorer southern states. However, these consequences of income redistribution policies are unavoidable. If the South is not paying its "fair share" of taxes and is receiving an unfair share of all federal benefits, the solution would seem to be a change in the tax laws and a reduction or redistribution of benefits, not the imposition of additional controls such as relocation rules which reduce production efficiency.

Furthermore, if the federal government simply collected taxes and channeled them back to the states in the form of equal outlays, government would not necessarily be acting efficiently. The cost of producing national defense, for example, may be lower in one region of the country than in another. If the federal government were required to allocate defense appropriations in proportion to the taxes collected in each region, defense would be more costly. The higher cost would then require the government either to accept a lower level of defense preparedness or to collect more taxes to develop a given level of defense preparedness. Alternately, if the government attempted to solve the "misallocation" of federal funds via restrictions on business mobility, production inefficiencies would result in the private as well as the public economy, the aggregate national income level would be lower, and the federal government would have to raise tax rates to finance any given defense posture. The higher tax rates could spell greater production inefficiencies across regions.

3

The Case for Relocation
Rules Continued

In the last chapter this study of the case for relocation rules was initiated by reviewing data on population and migration patterns, per capita income, and federal taxes and expenditures by regions. This chapter extends the analysis with an examination of the influence which business movements have had on regional employment opportunities. The study concludes with an examination of the major economic causes of business movements from the North.

Regional Employment Shifts

In making the case for relocation rules, Edward Kelly points out that the prosperity of the North and Midwest has been dependent upon an established industrial sector. He adds, "The corporate exodus from the industrial states is part of a national problem affecting the entire domestic economy: total manufacturing employment has stagnated, remaining in the range between 18 and 20 million jobs since the 1960s. In 1965 employment was approximately 18 million; now, twelve years later, it is only 18.5 million." Kelly points to the movement of northern manufacturing plants overseas and South as the cause of economic stagnation in the North:

> Domestic economic stagnation, largely caused by overseas investment of multinational corporations, is the context for the regional shift to the South now occurring. . . . Within the domestic economy, much of the shift has taken place since 1960. Between 1960 and 1975 manufacturing employment increased by 67.3 percent in the Southwest compared with 3.2 percent in the Great Lakes region and a loss of 13.7 percent in the Midwest and 9 percent in New England (Census Bureau regions). Within these regions, those states

TABLE 9

NONAGRICULTURAL EMPLOYEES, BY INDUSTRY, 1965–JANUARY 1978
(thousands)

		Goods-Producing			
Year	Total	Total goods	Mining	Contract construction	Manufacturing
1965	60,815	21,880	632	3,186	18,062
1966	63,955	23,116	627	3,275	19,214
1967	65,857	23,268	613	3,208	19,447
1968	67,951	23,693	606	3,306	19,781
1969	70,442	24,311	619	3,525	20,167
1970	70,920	23,507	623	3,536	19,349
1971	71,222	22,820	609	3,659	18,572
1972	73,714	23,546	625	3,831	19,090
1973	76,896	24,727	644	4,015	20,068
1974	78,413	24,697	694	3,957	20,046
1975	77,051	22,603	745	3,512	18,347
1976	79,443	23,332	783	3,594	18,956
1977	82,142	24,229	831	3,844	19,554
January 1978	82,554	23,972	695	3,528	19,749

			Service-Producing		
		Transport and public utilities	Wholesale and retail trade		
Year	Total services		Subtotal	Wholesale trade	Retail trade
1965	38,930	4,036	12,716	3,312	9,404
1966	40,839	4,151	13,245	3,437	9,808
1967	42,589	4,261	13,606	3,525	10,081
1968	44,258	4,311	14,099	3,611	10,488
1969	46,130	4,435	14,704	3,733	10,971
1970	47,412	4,504	15,040	3,816	11,225
1971	48,401	4,457	15,352	3,823	11,529
1972	50,167	4,517	15,975	3,943	12,032
1973	52,169	4,644	16,674	4,107	12,568
1974	53,715	4,696	17,017	4,223	12,794
1975	54,448	4,498	17,000	4,177	12,824
1976	56,111	4,509	17,694	4,263	13,431
1977	57,912	4,589	18,292	4,389	13,903
January 1978	58,582	4,582	18,532	4,455	14,077

TABLE 9 (CONTINUED)

Service-Producing

| Year | Finance, insurance, and coal estate | Government | | | Other services |
		Subtotal	Federal	State and local	
1965	3,023	10,074	2,378	7,696	9,087
1966	3,100	10,792	2,564	8,227	9,551
1967	3,225	11,398	2,719	8,679	10,099
1968	3,381	11,845	2,737	9,109	10,622
1969	3,562	12,202	2,758	9,444	11,228
1970	3,687	12,561	2,731	9,880	11,621
1971	3,802	12,887	2,696	10,192	11,903
1972	3,943	13,340	2,684	10,656	12,392
1973	4,091	13,739	2,663	11,075	13,021
1974	4,208	14,177	2,724	11,453	13,617
1975	4,223	14,720	2,748	11,973	14,006
1976	4,316	14,948	2,733	12,215	14,644
1977	4,508	15,190	3,737	12,463	15,353
January 1978	4,588	15,469	2,711	12,758	15,411

SOURCE: U.S. Bureau of Labor Statistics, *Employment and Earnings*, April 1978, table B–1.

with the most industry were the most vulnerable to the corporate shift. For example, highly industrialized Ohio, with 1,471,000 manufacturing jobs in 1969 (35 percent of the total state employment compared with 25 percent nationally), lost more than 150,000 of these jobs in the last eight years.[1]

Citing the Kelly study, *Business Week* added emphasis to its continuing report on the regional employment shifts with the midpage caption, "A loss of 1.4 million jobs in the North since 1966. Work goes south and west."[2]

Table 9 illustrates a point to be remembered when interpreting employment data over a span of years. The picture that is painted

[1] Edward Kelly, *Industrial Exodus: Public Strategies for Control of Runaway Plants* (Washington, D.C.: Conference for Alternative State and Local Public Policies, October 1977), pp. 1–2.
[2] "A New Layer of Structural Unemployment," *Business Week*, November 14, 1977, p. 144.

TABLE 10

REGIONAL EMPLOYMENT, BY INDUSTRY, 1972 AND 1978
(employment in thousands)

Industry	Northeast			North Central			Northeast and North Central Combined (percent change)
	1972	1978	Percent change	1972	1978	Percent change	
Total	14,565	16,912	+16	19,262	22,710	+18	+17
Mining	9	77	+756	102	168	+65	+120
Construction	542	419	−23	688	575	−16	−20
Manufacturing	3,542	5,142	+45	4,638	4,144	−11	+14
Transport and public utilities	896	605	−33	1,153	840	−17	−29
Wholesale and retail trade	3,067	3,350	+9	4,184	5,047	+20	+16
Finance, insurance, real estate	995	1,064	+7	904	1,056	+17	+12
Services	2,700	3,163	+17	2,970	3,875	+30	+24
Government	2,467	2,731	+10	3,382	3,823	+13	+12

Industry	South			West			South and West Combined (percent change)
	1972	1978	Percent change	1972	1978	Percent change	
Total	25,680	30,082	+17	10,726	12,319	+15	+16
Mining	386	336	−13	93	128	+33	− 3
Construction	1,397	1,819	+30	445	879	+98	+46
Manufacturing	8,035	7,812	−3	2,066	2,348	+14	+1
Transport and public utilities	1,606	2,578	+60	692	579	−16	+37
Wholesale and retail trade	5,440	6,926	+27	2,432	3,219	+32	+29
Finance, insurance, real estate	1,220	1,552	+27	594	787	+32	+29
Services	3,942	5,354	+36	1,948	2,748	+41	+38
Government	5,125	5,194	+21	2,402	2,840	+18	+20

NOTE: Employment figures are for the month of January in both 1972 and 1978.
SOURCE: U.S. Bureau of Labor Statistics, *Employment and Earnings*, vol. 25, no. 11 (March 1978), table B–8.

of the number of jobs lost or gained in the economy as a whole, in a region, or in an industrial group depends upon the years selected for comparison. From 1965 to 1974 total nonagricultural employment in the U.S. economy grew consistently, though more rapidly in some years than in others. As Table 9 shows, however, there were obvious ups and downs in the level of employment in the major subdivisions of employment. For instance, employment in goods-producing industries went up from 1965 to 1969, then receded to a low in 1971; it rose again from 1971 through 1974 and fell temporarily during 1975. Cyclical employment swings in goods industries have been offset in the aggregate employment figures by the strong and steady growth of employment in service-producing industries.

Employment in manufacturing industries is notable for its strong cyclical movements that in fact account for almost all the cyclical swings of employment in the overall goods-producing category. A comparison of manufacturing employment in 1970 with that in 1975 suggests that there was a significant downward trend in the number of jobs in that sector. Employment in manufacturing during that period decreased by 5 percent in contrast to upward employment trends in other sectors. As Kelly suggests, however, employment in manufacturing over the long run has actually remained fairly level. In short, the number of jobs said to be lost in manufacturing—or, for that matter, in any other sector of the economy—can be amplified or dampened by appropriate selection of the base year.

Furthermore, the employment picture of a region can be distorted by narrowing or widening the industrial group or the size of the regions covered. A favorite strategy of proponents of restrictions on business movement is to focus attention on the area of employment that has had the worst record and not to mention offsetting employment trends in other sectors of the economy.

Table 10 contains regional employment data by industry. From that table, it is clear that the North Central region had a marked decline (11 percent) in manufacturing employment from January 1972 to January 1978.[3] But the region was not as depressed as this figure alone would suggest. There were strong employment gains in mining (65 percent increase), wholesale and retail trade (20 percent increase), and services (30 percent increase). On balance, total employment in the North Central went up by 18 percent.

Overall employment in the Northeast rose by 16 percent, slightly

---

[3] These dates were chosen because the 1978 data were the latest available and because the two dates appeared to be in approximately the same phase of their respective business cycles.

less than the gains of the North Central and the South (17 percent increase) but more than the percentage employment gains of the West (15 percent increase). Note that between the dates covered by the table, manufacturing employment in the Northeast rose by 45 percent. Though construction, transportation, and utilities suffered employment losses during the period, the Northeast made strong employment gains in mining (756 percent increase) and services (17 percent increase). On the other hand, manufacturing employment in the South went down by 3 percent between the two dates, but employment in other areas rose significantly. These findings are not what one would expect after listening to advocates of relocation rules.

Of course, employment shifts in the northern industrial tier appear more drastic if the focus is changed from large geographical regions to their smaller subdivisions. Employment shifts can also be dramatized by drawing attention to the economic and personal distress that results when individual companies close down or move. In making the case for restrictions on business mobility, proponents have drawn attention to employment swings within small regional subdivisions of states and within one employment sector, manufacturing. They have largely ignored the beneficial and offsetting employment effects of a dynamic economy that gives way to changes in consumer preferences, income, technologies, labor market conditions, and government policies.

Finally, the loss of employment opportunities in any region can rarely be attributed to a single cause such as the migration of industry. Juxtaposing discussions of industrial migration with data on aggregate employment losses within a region gives a distorted impression of the economic hardship caused by the movement of industry. Regional employment patterns change because of changes within the region—deaths of firms, births of new firms, and expansions and contractions of old firms—as well as industry migration. To illustrate, consider Tables 11 and 12, which contain the results of a study conducted by Peter Allaman and David Birch on the gains and losses of employment in the northern industrial tier and the sunbelt. Table 11 reveals that during the 1969–1972 period slightly more than 70 percent of the employment gain in the North was caused by the expansion of existing firms, and more than 28 percent was the result of the establishment of new firms. More important for the purpose of this study, only 1.5 percent of the employment losses in the North from 1969 to 1972 were the result of the out-migration of business. The overwhelming majority of employment loss, 98.5 percent, was caused by the death or contraction of existing firms. Table 11 also shows

TABLE 11

CAUSES OF EMPLOYMENT GAINS AND LOSSES WITHIN REGIONS, DECEMBER 31, 1969–DECEMBER 31, 1972

Region	Total Employment Gains	Causes of Employment Gains (percent)			Total Employment Losses	Causes of Employment Losses (percent)		
		Births of new firms[a]	Expansion of firms	In-migration of firms		Deaths of firms[b]	Contraction of firms	Out-migration of firms
Northern industrial tier	3,516,603	28.6	70.1	1.3	4,672,977	53.8	44.7	1.5
New England	419,614	30.4	68.9	0.7	660,934	53.4	45.8	0.8
East North Central	1,599,179	28.7	70.4	0.9	1,976,375	53.6	45.8	0.7
Middle Atlantic	1,497,810	27.9	70.1	2.0	2,035,668	54.3	43.2	2.6
Sunbelt	2,634,250	34.5	64.3	1.2	2,570,544	57.0	42.5	0.4
South Atlantic	1,206,301	34.5	63.9	1.6	1,172,641	56.5	43.1	0.4
East South Central	543,436	32.5	66.7	0.5	518,122	59.2	40.3	0.5
West South Central	884,513	35.8	63.4	0.8	879,781	56.5	43.1	0.5

[a] "The appearance in the 1972 title of a firm with a new DUNS number, for which the year started was 1970–1972" (p. 4 of source).
[b] "The disappearance from the title of a firm with a particular DUNS number" (p. 4 of source).

SOURCE: Peter M. Allaman and David L. Birch, "Components of Employment Change for States by Industry Gross, 1970–1972," Joint Center for Urban Studies of M.I.T. and Harvard University, September 1975. The study uses Dun and Bradstreet data, as found in C. L. Jusenius and L. C. Ledebur, *A Myth in the Making: The Southern Economic Challenge and the Northern Economic Decline* (Washington, D.C.: U.S. Department of Commerce, Economic Development Administration, November 1976), p. 27.

TABLE 12

EMPLOYMENT CHANGE, BY REGION, DECEMBER 31, 1969–DECEMBER 31, 1972

Region	Total Employment 1969	Net Change 1969–1972 (percent)	Employment Change, as a Percent of 1969 Employment, Attributable to:					
			Birth of new firms[a]	Deaths of firms[b]	Expansion of firms	Contraction of firms	In-migration of firms	Out-migration of firms
North industrial tier	22,117,930	−1,129,933 (−5.1)	4.5	−11.4	11.2	−9.4	0.2	−0.3
New England	2,772,286	−214,846 (−7.8)	4.6	−12.7	10.4	−10.9	0.1	−0.2
East North Central	10,054,259	−379,890 (−3.8)	4.6	−10.5	11.2	−9.0	0.1	−0.1
Middle Atlantic	9,291,385	−535,197 (−5.8)	4.5	−11.9	11.3	−9.5	0.3	−0.6
Sunbelt	11,720,065	67,654 (0.6)	7.8	−12.5	14.5	−9.3	0.3	−0.1
South Atlantic	5,343,026	36,490 (0.7)	7.8	−12.4	14.4	−9.5	0.4	−0.1
East South Central	2,452,959	25,931 (1.1)	7.2	−12.6	14.8	−8.5	0.2	−0.1
West South Central	3,924,080	5,233 (0.1)	8.1	−12.7	14.3	−9.7	0.2	−0.1
U.S. Total	45,339,792	−1,314,854 (−2.9)	5.9	−12.1	12.7	−9.6	0.3	−0.2

[a] See note a, Table 11. [b] See note b, Table 11. SOURCE: Same as Table 11.

TABLE 13

AVERAGE EMPLOYEE COMPENSATION IN COTTON AND SYNTHETIC TEXTILES,
UNITED STATES, NORTHEAST, AND SOUTH, 1973

Compensation Item	United States		Northeast		South	
	% of compensation	$ per hour	% of compensation	$ per hour	% of compensation	$ per hour
Cotton textiles,						
total compensation	100.0	3.55	100.0	5.55	100.0	3.49
Pay for time worked	84.2	2.99	80.8	4.49	84.4	2.94
Pay for leave time						
(except sick leave)	4.3	0.15	7.4	0.41	4.1	0.14
Employer expenditures						
Retirement programs	7.4	0.26	6.8	0.37	7.4	0.26
Life insurance and						
health benefits[a]	2.8	0.10	3.4	0.19	2.8	0.10
Unemployment						
benefits	0.8	0.03	1.8	0.10	0.7	0.03
Nonproduction bonuses	0.5	0.02	—	—	0.5	0.02
Savings and thrift plans	0.1	*	—	—	0.1	*
Wages and salaries						
(gross payroll)[b]	89.0	3.16	88.3	4.90	89.0	3.11
Supplements to wages						
and salaries[c]	11.0	0.39	11.7	0.65	11.0	0.38
Synthetic textiles,						
total compensation	100.0	3.61	100.0	4.08	100.0	3.53
Pay for time worked	84.8	3.06	81.9	3.34	85.4	3.02
Pay for leave time						
(except sick leave)	4.1	0.15	5.1	0.21	3.9	0.14
Employer expenditures						
Retirement programs	6.9	0.25	6.0	0.25	7.1	0.25
Life insurance and						
health benefits[a]	2.9	0.10	4.2	0.17	2.6	0.09
Unemployment						
benefits	0.9	0.03	1.7	0.07	0.7	0.03
Nonproduction bonuses	0.4	0.01	0.9	0.04	0.3	0.01
Savings and thrift plans	*	*	0.1	*	*	*
Wages and salaries						
(gross payroll)[b]	89.4	3.23	88.1	3.59	89.7	3.17
Supplements to wages						
and salaries[c]	10.6	0.38	11.9	0.48	10.3	0.36

that only 1.2 percent of the South's employment gain was the result of the in-migration of businesses.

Table 12 expresses employment gain and loss in the northern industrial tier and sunbelt as a percentage of the 1969 employment levels in those regions. It shows that employment loss from the out-migration of firms from the North amounted to just 0.3 percent of total 1969 employment. The death and contraction of existing firms were far more important in determining the employment losses of the industrial states. In short, unless the experience of the last few years is dramatically different from the experience of 1969–1972, the data in Tables 11 and 12 suggest that proposals designed to remedy regional employment problems by restricting business out-migration would have very little effect in improving overall employment opportunities. The benefits of restrictions are likely to be more cosmetic and political than substantive. At best, the legislation would deal with the symptoms, rather than the underlying causes, of northern economic troubles.

Economic Causes of Industry Movement South

The reasons for the economic health of the South and West relative to the North cannot be fully dismissed or rationalized away and should be matters of concern for northern states. These reasons can be discussed under the headings of wages, unions, and taxes.

NOTES TO TABLE 13

[a] Includes other health benefit programs, principally state temporary disability insurance, not presented separately.

[b] Wages and salaries include all direct payments to workers. They consist of pay for time worked; pay for vacations, holidays, sick leave, and civic and personal leave; severance pay; and nonproduction bonuses.

[c] Supplements to wages and salaries include all employer expenditures for compensation other than for wages and salaries. They consist of expenditures for retirement programs (including direct pay to pensioners under pay-as-you-go private pension plans); expenditures for health benefit programs (except sick leave); expenditures for unemployment benefit programs (except severance pay); payments to vacation and holiday funds; and payments to savings and thrift plans.

NOTE: Because of rounding, sums of individual items may not equal totals. Dash (—) indicates zero. Asterisk (*) indicates less than $0.005 or less than .05 percent. The hourly compensation figures are based on all hours employed, not just hours worked.

SOURCE: James A. Morris and Thomas N. Schaap, *Economic Growth Trends in South Carolina* (Columbia, S.C.: University of South Carolina, Bureau of Business and Economic Research, 1977), p. 29.

Wages. In assessing the causes for firms' moving out of the North, Donovan Dennis, vice president of Fantus Corporation, a plant-relocation consulting firm, has said, "Labor costs are the big thing, far and away. Nine out of 10 times you can hang it on labor costs and unionization."[4] In many locations and in terms of many job classifications, southern states have a significant wage advantage over the Northeast and North Central regions in industries not requiring high skill levels. Table 13 compares 1973 wages in the Northeast and the South for two manufacturing processes, cotton and synthetic textiles. The total hourly compensation for all U.S. workers in cotton textiles averaged $3.55 in 1973; for workers in the Northeast it was $5.55; for workers in the South, $3.49. The hourly compensation in the North in that one manufacturing process was on average 59 percent higher than in the South. Although the gap between the synthetic industries in the Northeast and South is much smaller, there was in 1973 a similar pattern of compensation: average compensation in the Northeast ($4.08) was about 16 percent higher than in the South ($3.53). Furthermore, evidence on the value added per employee suggests that the gap between output per worker-hour in the North and the South has been closing and that textile workers in the South are now only slightly less productive than textile workers in other parts of the country.[5] Slightly lower productivity combined with significantly lower wage rates spell lower production costs for the final product in the South.

Although low-paid textile workers can be attracted to other industries moving South, it does not follow that wages in all other industries will be as low, relative to the Northeast, as they are in textiles; nor does it necessarily follow that southern manufacturing workers, taken as a group, are worse off, in terms of real income, than their counterparts in the North. Table 14 portrays by region the 1974 wages of workers in several occupations, such as carpenter and janitor, expressed as a percentage of the U.S. average wage for each occupational group. The hourly compensation of workers in the North Central region was significantly above the wage rate in the South in every occupational group listed. In the North Central region, carpenters, for example, received 106 percent of the national average wage, whereas in the South they received 96 percent. Note, however,

---

[4] Donovan Dennis, as originally quoted in *Akron Beacon Journal*, February 29, 1971, and requoted in Kelly, *Industrial Exodus*, p. 3.

[5] James A. Morris and Thomas N. Schaap, *Economic Growth Trends in South Carolina* (Columbia, S.C.: University of South Carolina, Bureau of Business and Economic Research, 1977), p. 28.

TABLE 14

Earnings in Selected Blue-Collar Manufacturing Occupations as Percentage of U.S. Average, 1962 and 1974

Year and Region	Maintenance and Toolroom						Custodial and Material Movement				
	Carpenter	Electrician	Machinist	Auto mechanic	Painter	Tool and die	Janitor	Laborer	Order filler	Truck driver	Forklift operator
1962											
Northeast	96	96	96	102	94	93	96	100	98	100	99
North Central	104	103	103	104	103	106	107	107	105	105	104
South	99	98	99	87	100	98	84	81	84	78	87
West	104	104	105	108	104	100	107	107	111	106	105
Standard deviation of regional percentages	3.9	3.9	4.0	9.2	4.5	5.4	11.0	12.3	11.6	14.5	8.3
1974											
Northeast	94	93	96	99	93	91	96	97	101	106	96
North Central	106	106	104	106	106	105	110	110	107	108	107
South	96	93	95	85	98	88	84	83	86	77	84
West	104	103	107	111	100	98	100	105	96[a]	114	104
Standard deviation of regional percentages	5.9	6.8	5.9	11.3	5.4	7.6	10.8	11.8	8.9	16.5	10.3

[a] At late as 1972, earnings in the West were above the U.S. average.

NOTE: Earnings are hourly earnings excluding premium pay for overtime, holidays, and late shifts.

SOURCE: U.S. Bureau of Labor Statistics, *Handbook of Labor Statistics, 1975*, Reference edition, table 109, as taken from Lynn E. Growne, "How Different Are Regional Wages?" *New England Economic Review*, January–February 1978, p. 40.

TABLE 15

COMPARISON OF AVERAGE HOURLY EARNINGS IN MANUFACTURING, 1975
(dollars)

Region	Unadjusted Earnings	Standardized for Cost of Living
United States	4.81	4.81
Northeast		
New England	4.42	4.03
Middle Atlantic	4.93	4.73
North Central		
East North Central	5.60	5.54
West North Central	4.92	5.07
South		
South Atlantic	3.95	4.11
East South Central	4.07	4.47
West South Central	4.45	4.94
West		
Mountain	4.70	4.95
Pacific	5.31	5.09

SOURCE: Same as Table 14.

that the relative wage of carpenters in the South was greater than in the Northeast where they got 94 percent of the national average. On the other hand, the average compensation in every other occupation except for painters and electricians was greater in the Northeast than in the South.

The average hourly earnings for all manufacturing employees in 1975, unadjusted for cost-of-living differences, are presented in Table 15. Businesses are concerned with the actual dollar wages they pay because they affect directly the dollar cost of producing their products. Table 15 clearly reveals that, on average, the unadjusted hourly dollar cost of labor in all subdivisions of the Northeast is higher than in the South. (It should be recognized that those wage rates are not standardized for differences in the industrial composition of manufacturing and differences in the skill mix.) Although the regional wage gap is not as stark as it is in textiles, many (but by no means all) businesses definitely have a wage incentive to incur relocation costs when the difference in hourly labor cost is greater than the difference in skill. The table also reveals that, after adjustment is made for the South's lower cost of living, southern manufacturing workers are not *all* worse off than their northern colleagues. The real wage rate of manufacturing workers on average throughout the

South is higher than that in the New England area. Still, most real manufacturing wages are higher in most areas of the country than in the South, and rudimentary evidence is presented in the following section to explain why some firms and individual workers choose to move from one region to another.

Although business movement South is commonly explained, as I have done, in terms of the "wage attraction" of the South, it is more illuminating to examine business movement as a consequence of the "wage push" in the North. This change in perspective is comparable to calling a glass half full rather than half empty, and it can change one's view of social conditions and the economic consequences of industry relocation. From the wage-attraction perspective, one may conclude that "low-paid serfs in the South" are causing economic harm to the North. In contrast, the wage-push perspective suggests that wages in the North are higher and on the rise for some economic reason, such as competition for workers from the developing service sector in the North. Manufacturers are forced to pay higher wages or their labor force will be pulled away by expanding companies in other sectors. The industry that moves South is thus "pushed" South by competition for the labor resources in the North. From this perspective, industrial movement South, either slight or substantial, is a consequence of gains made by many workers in the North, and the case for restriction of business relocation becomes a case for the retardation of economic growth and development of the North. Restrictions on business mobility will tend to keep resources fixed in place and unavailable for use in expanding, economically more beneficial, industry.[6] It is an attempt to keep lower paying jobs and to keep people in lower productivity work. This will be discussed further in Chapter 4.

Unions. When responding to questions "on the record," businessmen tend to put wages and unions at the bottom of any list of reasons for moving South.[7] "Off the record," however, they often admit that unions or "better labor-management relations" (a euphemism for "getting out from under union domination") is a prime reason for their decision to move.

In the North, the percentage of nonfarm labor that was unionized varied in 1974 from a high of 38 percent in Michigan to a low of

[6] As argued in the next chapter, restrictions on business mobility can only slow the movement of labor and other resources to the expanding sector.

[7] A. Stanley Austin and Ray C. Roberts, Jr., "The Effects of Wage Levels on Decisions to Locate Manufacturing Facilities in South Carolina," University of South Carolina, *Business and Economic Review* (October 1973), pp. 2–10.

little more than 24 percent in Massachusetts. In the South, the state with the highest percentage of its work force belonging to a union was Alabama (about 19 percent). In contrast, only 6.9 percent of nonfarm workers in North Carolina were members of unions in 1974 (see Table 16). In 1974 right-to-work laws were nonexistent in the northern industrial tier; whereas in the South and Southwest, except in Kentucky, Louisiana, and New Mexico, right-to-work laws were in force. The presence or absence of right-to-work laws is an index of the power of unions to influence state legislatures and to obtain legislation, such as generous workers' compensation and unemployment compensation laws, that can cause high costs in some industries without sufficient benefits to workers to make those industries commensurately more attractive to labor.

Many businesses understandably want to move away from unions. A substantial body of economic research shows that unions are responsible for wages being anywhere from 5 to 25 percent higher in unionized shops than in nonunionized shops.[8] The average increase found by various studies is about 10 percent. Further, many business executives argue that unions tend to complicate the production process, slowing the decision-making process and causing management to retain a higher percentage of inefficient and lackadaisical workers. All of this adds to the costs of production and makes successful competition and a firm's long-run survival uncertain. In short, the absence of unions and the cultural bias against them in the South have given southern states a competitive advantage, however small.

The absence of a highly unionized South has also benefited the nonunion section of the labor force in the North. The threat of businesses' moving South in response to union wage demands has kept unions in the North from pushing up wages as much as they otherwise would have. This, in turn, has kept the prices of goods and services lower than they would have been in the absence of a nonunion South. The nonunion South has, accordingly, contributed to the standard of living of workers in the North, especially nonunion workers.[9]

---

[8] For a brief review of the literature on the effects of unions on wages and employment, see F. Ray Marshall, Allan M. Cartter, and Allan G. King, *Labor Economics: Wages, Employment and Trade Unionism* (Homewood, Ill.: Richard D. Irwin, 1976), chap. 14.

[9] Union success in pushing wage rates above free-market levels in some industries causes a decline in wage rates in other industries, because restrictions on job opportunities in unionized industries force workers to seek jobs in other industries. See Stephen Sobotka, *Profile of Michigan: Economic Trends and Paradoxes* (New York: Free Press of Glenencoe, Macmillan, 1963).

TABLE 16

Membership in National Unions as a Proportion of Employees in Nonagricultural Establishments, by State, 1974

State	Percent	State	Percent
All states	26.2	Missouri	32.3
Alabama[a]	19.1	Montana	25.7
Alaska	26.4	Nebraska[a]	15.1
Arizona[a]	16.0	Nevada[a]	27.4
Arkansas[a]	16.8	New Hampshire	15.1
California	28.2	New Jersey	28.2
Colorado	18.9	New Mexico	14.1
Connecticut	25.1	New York	38.0
Delaware	20.1	North Carolina[a]	6.9
Florida[a]	12.5	North Dakota	15.1
Georgia[a]	14.5	Ohio	33.2
Hawaii	36.2	Oklahoma	15.0
Idaho	15.5	Oregon	26.5
Illinois	34.9	Pennsylvania	37.5
Indiana	33.2	Rhode Island	27.3
Iowa[a]	21.2	South Carolina[a]	8.0
Kansas[a]	14.1	South Dakota[a]	11.0
Kentucky	25.1	Tennessee[a]	18.7
Louisiana	16.3	Texas[a]	13.0
Maine	16.2	Utah[a]	14.9
Maryland-District of		Vermont	17.7
Columbia	21.6	Virginia[a]	13.8
Massachusetts	24.4	Washington	36.7
Michigan	38.4	West Virginia	38.2
Minnesota	25.3	Wisconsin	28.7
Mississippi[a]	12.0	Wyoming[a]	18.2

[a] State has right-to-work law.

NOTE: Based on reports from 129 national unions and estimates for forty-six. Also included are local unions directly affiliated with the AFL-CIO and members in single-firm and local unaffiliated unions. Excludes employee associations.

SOURCE: U.S. Bureau of the Census, *Directory of National Unions and Employee Associations, 1975*, bulletin 1937 (1977), p. 74.

Taxes. State and local taxes in 1975 were one-third higher in the Northeast as a percentage of per capita income than they were in the South. As shown in Table 17, there is substantial variation in the tax rates of both the North and the South; but the general tendency is clear: taxes are higher in the traditional industrial states than in the faster growing southern region. New York collected taxes in 1975 that averaged 15.7 percent of per capita personal income; at the other extreme, Alabama taxes averaged 9 percent of per capita personal income. As a consequence, the residents of Alabama had, on average, a state and local tax advantage over New Yorkers of about 75 percent. Conversely, residents of Ohio, a highly industrialized state, paid taxes at an overall rate lower than that in several southern states.

Higher taxes and tax rates do not necessarily detract from an industry's evaluation of a site. Higher taxes can mean greater availability and higher quality of public services. Such services can reduce the cost of doing business. High taxes are a detraction when they are disproportionately levied on business or when the revenue collected is inefficiently used in providing public services. There are several reasons for believing that, like unions and wages, some tax structures in the North are "pushing" industry out of the region. First, many firms can divide their functions between different locations. Production plants can be established in the South where low taxes benefit employees as well as the firms themselves, and offices can be located in northern urban areas, where firms can selectively take advantage of the public benefits offered by states with relatively higher taxes.

Second, a growing volume of literature in public choice economics reveals a tendency toward diseconomies of scale in government at all levels:[10] with growth in tax collections, the quantity and quality of public services do not rise proportionately. The average cost of services provided is, therefore, disproportionately higher in states with higher tax rates. Many businesses have an incentive to move South, to smaller governmental units with lower tax rates. Alternately, they may move to another state in the North with relatively lower tax rates. New Hampshire is being called the "northern sunbelt state" because its low taxes are causing an influx of industry.[11]

Third, where state and local tax rates are lower and public services are on average provided more efficiently, the supply of labor at any given money wage will be higher, and the wages that must be paid will be lower. The lower tax rates indirectly give businesses a competitive cost advantage over firms in higher tax rate districts.

Fourth, when taxes are used to provide income supplements for strikers and people who do not want to work, a practice in wider use

---

[10] See, for example, Thomas E. Borcherding, *Budgets and Bureaucrats: The Sources of Government Growth* (Durham, N.C.: Duke University Press, 1977).

[11] David Gumpert, "Northern Nirvana: 'New' New Hampshire Finds that Low Taxes Help to Fuel Economy," *Wall Street Journal*, May 25, 1978, p. 1.

TABLE 17

Region and State	Taxes per Capita (dollars)	Taxes as Percent of per Capita Personal Income
Northeast	814	13.0
New England	727	12.1
Maine	571	12.0
New Hampshire	525	9.7
Vermont	699	14.3
Massachusetts	814	13.5
Rhode Island	645	11.2
Connecticut	697	10.2
Middle Atlantic	843	13.2
New York	1,025	15.7
New Jersey	725	10.7
Pennsylvania	636	10.8
North Central	648	12.2
East North Central	639	11.8
Ohio	534	9.2
Indiana	580	10.4
Illinois	730	10.8
Michigan	682	11.4
Wisconsin	533	9.5
West North Central	617	10.8
Minnesota	754	13.1
Iowa	637	10.8
Missouri	523	9.6
North Dakota	613	10.3
South Dakota	543	10.8
Nebraska	577	9.8
Kansas	598	10.0
South		
South Atlantic	549	10.0
Delaware	697	10.7
Maryland	728	11.5
District of Columbia	759	10.3
Virginia	563	9.7
West Virginia	533	10.8
North Carolina	485	9.8
South Carolina	446	9.6
Georgia	508	10.1
Florida	521	9.3

(Table continues on next page.)

TABLE 17 (CONTINUED)

Region and State	Taxes per Capita (dollars)	Taxes as Percent of per Capita Personal Income
East South Central	453	9.7
Kentucky	497	10.2
Tennessee	451	9.3
Alabama	415	9.0
Mississippi	446	11.0
West South Central	509	9.6
Arkansas	405	9.0
Louisiana	566	11.7
Oklahoma	482	9.2
Texas	515	9.2
West	770	12.4
Mountain	614	11.2
Montana	612	11.4
Idaho	528	10.2
Wyoming	697	11.5
Colorado	631	10.6
New Mexico	548	11.3
Arizona	658	12.3
Utah	506	10.4
Nevada	770	11.7
Pacific	823	12.7
Washington	676	10.8
Oregon	635	11.1
California	869	13.3
Alaska	842	8.9
Hawaii	852	12.8

SOURCE: U.S. Bureau of the Census, *Statistical Abstract of the United States* (Washington, D.C., 1977).

in the North than in the South,[12] employee attitudes toward work and management authority can change in a way that reduces production efficiency. According to reports, an important reason businesses move South is the belief that workers in the South are more firmly committed to "giving a day's labor for a day's pay" than their counterparts in the North.[13] On the other hand, when taxes are used for

[12] Tax Foundation, Inc., *Facts and Figures on Government Finance* (New York, 1977), tables 117 and 118.
[13] "Business Loves the Sunbelt (and Vice Versa)," *Business Week*, June 1977, pp. 132–146.

regional economic development programs, for employee training facilities, and in general for making service concessions to prospective businesses, production costs are lowered and taxes are an attraction. The use of state funds for luring business is a major concern of the proponents of business relocation rules. They want to put a stop to the competition for industry among governments: "In an attempt to tear down some of the fear and antagonism, states and cities should enter agreements among themselves specifying legitimate and illegitimate forms of competition for industry. As part of such an agreement, the practice and spirit of 'raiding' should be eliminated."[14]

Summary and Conclusions

The case for relocation rules is largely a collection of arguments that carry little force under close scrutiny. The level of business migration has been neither appreciable nor as large as has been claimed. The migration that has occurred has not had the dire employment consequences previously reported. Further, the North is not as economically depressed, relative to the South, as has been suggested or as may be inferred by looking only at the manufacturing sector of the northern economy. Changes in the northern service sector have more than compensated for any loss in manufacturing employment and have kept the mean standard of living in the North rising and above the standard of living in the South.

Much of the change in employment in agriculture and manufacturing occurring in the North is a consequence of the North's becoming relatively more developed and reaching higher income levels. At an earlier stage of development, demand for agricultural goods failed to rise as rapidly as productivity in agriculture because of a low income elasticity of demand, and employment in agriculture fell. Because demand for agricultural products lagged behind productivity and income, the increase in income was spent for other products and services. The demand for manufacturing products then rose more rapidly than productivity, and employment in manufacturing increased.[15]

Now the rise in productivity in some manufacturing industries in the North is beginning to outrun the rise in the demand for products.

---

[14] Kelly, *Industrial Exodus*, pp. 18 and 19.

[15] For a more complete discussion of the stages of economic development through which economies often pass, see Yale Brozen, *The Future of the Economy* (Chicago, Ill.: University of Chicago, Industrial Relations Center, 1963); and Yale Brozen, "Prospective Industrial Technology and the Labor Force in a Developing Economy" (Chicago, Ill.: University of Chicago, Graduate School of Business); processed.

Manufacturing employment in the North is stabilizing in some industries and sectors and falling in others. Employment in the North is now rising rapidly in services (such as education, finance, insurance, and medical care) and attracting people from manufacturing and agriculture. The comparative advantage that is developing in the service and the restructuring of occupations and industries in all regions of the country are beneficial consequences of a normal development process for a dynamic economy.

4
Markets and Regional Economic Adjustments

Markets enable people to buy and sell what they want at prices they freely choose to accept. They also enable people to adjust to changes in economic and social conditions. Markets are by no means perfect—there are costs involved—but they achieve a degree of efficiency and yield increasing per capita incomes because they give individuals private incentives to make adjustments to the requirements of others and to changes in available capital and technology. As Adam Smith wrote more than 200 years ago, each market participant, by pursuing his own interest, is led "to promote an end which was no part of his intention."[1] That end is the expansion of the national product and the satisfaction of consumers.

Competition is the acclaimed benefactor of markets because it forces people to reveal what they are willing to do. At the limit it forces them to reveal the *minimum* prices they are willing to accept for the products or labor services being sold and to reveal the *maximum* prices they are willing to offer for products or labor services they want to buy. Competition, to the extent that it exists in the marketplace, induces people to produce at their limits, given their preferences and cost constraints. In this sense competition maximizes national output and income. Government policies that restrict trade or the ability of markets to adjust to changes in preferences, prices, and profits restrict not only individual choices but also national production and income.

The purpose of this chapter is to explore on a conceptual level

[1] Adam Smith, *An Inquiry into the Nature and Causes of the Wealth of Nations,* Modern Library edition (New York: Random House, 1937), p. 423: "Consumption is the sole end and purpose of all production; and the interest of the producer ought to be attended to, only so far as it may be necessary for promoting that of the consumer."

the economic consequences of restrictions on business mobility. A general discussion of how markets work will illuminate some consequences of relocation rules, which are unsuspected and unintended by their advocates. In the following section, each economic effect of business relocation restrictions will be discussed separately, together with an explanation of its causes.

The Economic Consequences of Restrictions

• *Restrictions on business movements will retard the economic development of all regions of the country.*

People trade with one another in part because of the comparative advantages they have in production. A person who can produce a good efficiently will give up less in producing that good than someone who is not so efficient. Another way of saying the same thing is that a person who has a comparative advantage in production can produce a good more cheaply than others can. Therefore, if people produce those goods in which they have a comparative advantage and trade them for other things they want, production costs will be lower than they would be if everyone tried to be self-sufficient. And, since costs are reduced by specialization and exchanges, more output can be produced with the resources available to the community than would otherwise be possible.

When evaluating the economic consequences of relocation rules, two points must be kept in mind. First, people in different parts of the country have comparative advantages in different goods, and trade occurs between different parts of the country when people can gain from it. They receive a better deal by trading with others than by trying to produce all the goods they want by themselves. This is the reason people in the North trade with people in the South. They benefit from their exchanges because specialization results in reduced production costs and expanded output.

Second, the comparative advantages of people in different regions are continually changing because the conditions of production—the availability of resources, technology, and consumer preferences for work and goods—continually change. Changes in comparative advantage spell changes in relative costs. What was once relatively less costly to produce in the North can—because of a change in production technology, for example—become less costly to produce in the South. By moving from the North to the South, a firm can keep its costs of production less than they would be if production were not moved.

Regional shifts in comparative advantage may occur because a strategic resource used in making product A becomes relatively more scarce in one region than in another. Therefore, the cost of producing good A in one region rises above the cost of producing it in another region. In addition, increases in workers' educational level or the discovery of more abundant supplies of a given resource may reduce the cost of producing good B in a region where it was formerly not produced and thus cause the region to initiate or expand its production of B. Again, a shift in production within the region from A to B can keep the costs of production below what they would otherwise be. The industry that expands because of beneficial cost changes begins to impinge on the resources available to industries that once dominated the region. The costs of producing A in that region go up and, as a consequence, the production of A moves elsewhere. Finally, the preferences of people can change. An increase in the demand for services within a particular region, for example, may cause resources like labor to move from the manufacturing sector into the service sector, causing wages and production costs in the manufacturing sector to rise. One result of such a sequence of events may be that some manufacturing plants will release their labor to a growing economic sector and move to another location.

Describing the causes of changes in regional economic structures is difficult under the best of circumstances. This is because costs are based on people's subjective evaluation of goods, and those evaluations cannot be directly observed in the market process.[2] Several reasons can be identified, however, for changes in the comparative advantage of many sections of the North in recent decades. First, the demand for services in the North has increased more rapidly than in other parts of the country. Second, the advent of environmental legislation has placed more severe restrictions on production in the congested northern region than in many other parts of the country and has increased the relative cost of production in the North. The unavailability of "pollution rights" has caused many firms to decide on southern, less polluted locations. According to one report, a major reason the Volkswagen company chose Pennsylvania as the site of its first U.S. plant is that the state agreed to reduce its own pollution by using a more expensive paving process in road construction so that VW could have "pollution rights" to start up production.[3]

---

[2] James M. Buchanan, *Costs and Choice* (New York: Markham Publishers, 1969).
[3] Bruce Yandle, "The Emerging Market in Air Pollution Rights," *Regulation*, July/August 1978, pp. 21–29.

If ill-conceived environmental restrictions affect a region's comparative advantage, the region's income will be reduced and appropriate changes in the environmental laws are called for. If those laws cannot be changed, however, the solution to a region's economic woes is not to restrict business migration. Keeping some businesses from moving out will only cause the costs of production to be higher than they would otherwise be, given the existing environmental legislation, and the region's income will be restricted.

If the comparative advantage of a region changes for whatever reason, a restriction on business migration will keep resources tied up in the comparatively inefficient sector of the region. Firms in that sector will be forced to retain employees and other resources that could be utilized more effectively in another sector. A sector that should be expanding because of its comparative advantage will be restricted from doing so because resources will not be released quickly from the relatively inefficient sector. In summary, governmental rules that impede the movement of manufacturing industry out of the North will retard not only the development of the manufacturing industry in the South but also the development of the expanding service sector in the North. Furthermore, restrictions on business mobility will cause production costs to be higher than they would otherwise be and, to that extent, will reduce national production and income.

• *If the movement of manufacturing firms from the North is restricted by legislation, the movement of manufacturing jobs to the South will be impeded but not stopped.*

Firms are willing to incur the costs of relocation because the move enables them to protect their competitive position or to gain competitive advantages over their market rivals—that is, the costs of production are lower in the new location than in the old. If firms are unable to move to new, more profitable locations in the South, then the profitable opportunities there will be exploited by others. Restrictions on business mobility will cause new firms to spring up in the South and existing southern firms to expand by more than they otherwise would. Because their costs of production are lower, emerging and expanding firms in the more profitable locations will be able to undersell firms that have remained where they are. Firms remaining in their old locations will eventually be forced to contract their operations or to go out of business. By way of births of new firms and deaths of old ones, the employment structure of regional economies will shift in the long run in spite of the relocation rules. Such rules will do little to slow the process and, because they will spur the formation of new firms, they will increase the cost of adjustment.[4]

• *Restrictions on business mobility will increase the power of unions.*

Unions are interested in raising wages and fringe benefits for their members. They know, however, that their ability to do this is restricted by the threat of firms moving to new locations. If businesses are prevented from moving, the immediate threat of job loss is taken away, and, as a consequence, unions can be expected to increase their demands on employers. The result will be even higher production costs in the less profitable locations. The benefits of relocation rules will be captured in the short-run income stream of union members.

• *Wages in many nonunionized labor markets will tend to fall (in relation to what they would have been) because of restrictions on business mobility.*

The supply of labor in any market is dependent upon both pecuniary and nonpecuniary factors: skill and education required, location, climate, risk of injury, and social prestige of the job. Because such factors affect the supply of labor in individual markets, they also influence the wage rate. Steeplejacks tend to make more than janitors because their skills are more difficult to acquire (which restricts the number of people who are able to do the job) and because of the risks associated with working on metal beams in high places. Ph.D. accountants teaching in universities tend to make less in money wages than their counterparts in private industry, but they receive the nonpecuniary benefits of flexibility in scheduling their time and of tenured employment (which has been described as a one-way lifetime contract).

The supply of labor in any market is also affected by an expectation that the firms in a regional industry will close down altogether or

---

[4] Under the proposed National Employment Priorities Act, the secretary of labor, with the advice of the National Employment Relocation Advisory Council, would have been empowered to keep a firm from relocating if the move is without "adequate justification." Presumably, this means that if a firm is deemed to be making a "fair rate of return on its investment," then it can be prevented from moving. As noted in Chapter 1, advocates of the proposal seem to be interested in stopping firms that want to move because of "economic greed." However, since expanded output in new locations will reduce the profitability in old locations, even firms that at first cannot provide "adequate justification" for a move eventually will be able to present the needed justification. What was once a move for so-called economic greed will become a move for economic necessity. Eventually, the government will find itself subsidizing firms that it wants to stay in their old locations.

move elsewhere. Generally, the greater the threat of a move, the higher the wage employees with given skills will demand before accepting employment in that industry. Restrictions on business mobility propose to reduce the threat of industrial movement, especially from the North. In the short-run, the effect will be to increase the relative attractiveness of employment and, hence, the supply of labor in markets from which firms might otherwise move. To the extent that those markets are competitive, the money wage rates will fall. If firms are forced to give severance pay, in competitive labor markets the relative attractiveness of employment and the supply of labor will increase further, pushing the money wage rates down lower. Of course, markets are not perfectly competitive and they do not always fully adjust to changes in the economic environment. The general tendency, however, is clear; money wages (as opposed to real wages) will tend to be depressed by labor supply responses. Though money wages may go up, they will not rise by as much as they otherwise would, because more people will want to work where the threat of employment loss in the near term is reduced. Workers who were once willing to accept the risk of losing their jobs in order to receive the higher money wage will no longer have that opportunity; their real income will definitely be reduced.

In the long run, new labor market equilibriums will be achieved as regional employment structures change to what they would have been in the absence of the relocation rules. On balance, however, the country will be poorer: relocation rules cause resources to be inefficiently allocated among regions and fewer goods and services to be produced. In other words, the per capita income of the country will be restricted; that is, if it grows, it will grow by less than otherwise because of the relocation rules.

- *Relocation rules will cause wealth transfers and losses.*

When people invest in businesses they are actually buying a bundle of legal rights. The market value of those rights is equal to the present value of the future income stream that can be received by holding onto those rights. Many people have invested in businesses (either directly through the purchase of plant and equipment or indirectly through the purchase of stocks and bonds), assuming that they have purchased not only the "right" to operate the business but also the "right" to move the business to any location they perceive to be more profitable. On this assumption, they paid more for the business or the stock than they otherwise would have.

Since relocation rules propose to take the right of movement

58

away from business owners, they are in effect proposing to reduce the income stream of the business and the wealth of business owners. Because under the proposed National Employment Priorities Act government would have been able to prevent certain moves, the demand for the assets of a firm that would otherwise choose to move will be reduced; the value of those assets will also be reduced. Alternately, because under relocation rules firms cannot move as readily to seek out profitable opportunities, the demand for and the market price of stock of companies that would otherwise move will be reduced. Consequently, relocation rules will cause a transfer of wealth away from owners of businesses. A part of that wealth will be transferred to owners of companies in other places, such as the South, that are able to emerge or expand and to survive more profitably because other businesses have had their movements impeded. Part of the wealth will simply be a deadweight loss because of the subsequent decrease in production efficiency. And part of the wealth transfers will be picked up by government agencies that will be expanded to increase government supervision over business decisions.

Although transferring wealth from one group to another may be a socially desirable goal, relocation rules seem like a particularly clumsy way of achieving such an objective. Many people who will lose wealth in the transfer process are small investors; many, in fact, are likely to be on retirement plans that are tied to the market prices of various stocks. If the value of these stocks goes down, then the prospective income from retirement programs will also fall. In short, it is doubtful that any analysis has been made to determine who will be harmed by the proposed legislation and by how much each person will be hurt.

• *Restrictions on business mobility will increase the monopoly power of state and local government.*

The framers of the Constitution attempted to place restraints on government by sharply defining its role and by introducing market principles into its organization. James Madison wrote in *The Federalist Papers*:

> In a single republic, all the power surrendered by the people is submitted to the administration of a single government; and the usurpations are guarded against by a division of the government into distinct and separate departments. In the *compound* republic of America, the power surrendered by the people is first divided between two distinct governments, and then the portion allotted to each subdivided among

distinct and separate departments. Hence a double security arises to the rights of people. The different governments will control each other, at the same time each will be controlled by itself.[5]

In short, Madison and others believed that the power of government could be constrained in part by competition among governments, that is, by market forces similar to those faced by private companies. If a company raises its price or lowers the quality of its product, it can expect to lose customers to competing firms which hold prices down or maintain quality or both. Similarly, a government which raises taxes or reduces the quantity or quality of its public services can expect to lose people and its tax base to other competing governments. Although the degree of potential competition among governments may be less than it is among private firms, to the extent that competition occurs among state and local governments it reduces their power to raise taxes and lower the quality of services provided.

Restrictions on business mobility will hinder the response of businesses to tax increases imposed by local governments. To the extent that this occurs, relocation restrictions increase the power of governments to raise taxes and reduce the quality of services they provide. Consequently, the enactment of relocation rules is likely to lead to higher taxes and lower quality services in many jurisdictions.

Summary and Conclusions

Restrictions on business mobility will increase production costs by reducing the efficiency with which resources are allocated on an inter- and intraregional basis. They will increase the bargaining power of unions, and to the extent that they impede businesses' ability to move into markets where production is more profitable, they will tend to reduce competition among businesses from different regions and foster local monopoly and monopsony power among existing producers. Because businesses will not be able to "vote with their feet" as easily as they would be able to in the absence of relocation rules, the monopoly power of local and state governments will be enhanced and will perhaps lead to higher tax prices for local and state government services. Granted, restrictions on business movement will affect income and wealth transfers, which may be a social objective of its proponents. However, relocation rules are a particularly haphazard

---

[5] James Madison, "The Social Foundation of Political Freedom," *The Federalist Papers*, no. 51 (New York: Washington Square Press, 1964), p. 122.

way of accomplishing such social objectives. The end result of the transfers may be the opposite of that planned by social engineers. After the political rhetoric is peeled away and the emotions of individual employment losses are set aside, restrictions on business mobility have very little to recommend them.